CONTENTS

INTRODUCTION

Hello and welcome to "Speak Hebrew like a Native"!

In order to become a fluent Hebrew speaker it's not enough to learn grammar and vocabulary. You need to know how native speakers build sentences and use them in their conversations. This book provides you with exactly that knowledge. It includes hundreds of customizable sentences that can be used in typical everyday situations.

With the help of this book you will be able to express yourself exactly like a Hebrew native speaker would. You will be able to speak with confidence, because you know that these sentences are correct and you will be more fluent, because you won't have to look for words or translate what you want to say from your native language into Hebrew.

The set-up of the book is not linear in its philosophy, but offers a broad range of topics. That's why you don't necessarily need to study one lesson after the other, but you can choose a lesson that is of interest and start right there.

You will notice that the English version of the Hebrew sentences is not always an exact translation. This is done in order to provide you with common expressions that a native Hebrew speaker would use, and sometimes a literal translation wouldn't sound natural. The meaning, however, will be the same.

For the best learning experience, it is recommended that you already know how to read Hebrew. However, I have included a phonetic transcription that will help you get the pronunciation right.

As for the conjugation of the verbs, if you'd like to modify the example phrases (e.g. feminine or plural forms), I recommend using an online verb conjugator such as http://pealim.com or http://conjugator.reverso.net/conjugation-hebrew.html.

And now I invite you to jump right into your first lesson and in less time than you expect you will speak Hebrew like a native!

SECTION 1: MAKING FRIENDS

1.1 STARTING A CONVERSATION

שלום, מה נשמע? הכל בסדר, תודה. מה איתך? גם בסדר.
Shalom, ma nishmah? Hakol beseder, todah. Ma itkhah? Gam beseder.
Hi, how are you? Good, thanks, and you? Also good!

שמי אבי. ואיך קוראים לך?
Shmee Avi. Ve'eykh kor'eem lakh (feminine) / lekha (masculine)?
My name's Avi. And what's your name?

קוראים לי מירב. נעים להכיר!
Kor'eem lee Meyrav. Na'eem lehakeer!
My name's Meyrav. Nice to meet you!

תזכיר / תזכירי לי איך קוראים לך?
Tazkeer (masc.) / Tazkeeri (fem.) lee eykh kor'eem lakh (fem.) / lekha (masc.)?
What was your name again?

אתם מכירים?
Atem mekeereem?
Do you guys know each other?

תכירו, זה אבי וזאת מירב.
Takeeru, ze Avi vezot Meyrav.
May I introduce you to each other? That's Avi, that's Meyrav.

נעים להכיר!
Na'eem lehakeer!
Nice to meet you!

1.2 RECEIVING GUESTS

אהלן! טוב שבאת!
Ahlan! Tov shebat (fem.) / shebata (masc.)
Hi! I'm so glad you could make it!

כנסי / כנס / כנסו!
Kanssee (fem.) / Kaness (masc.) / Kanssoo (group)
Please come in!

אתלה את המעיל.
Etleh et hame'eel.
I'll hang up the coat.

בדרך כלל לא כזה בלאגן פה.
Bederekh clal lo kazeh balagan po.
Usually it's not such a mess.

אפשר להציע משהו לשתות?
Efshar lehatseea mashehu lishtot?
May I offer you something to drink?

אפשר להציע משהו לאכול?
Efshar lehatseea mashehu le'ekhol?
May I offer you something to eat?

יש לי יין אדום, יין לבן, מיץ תפוזים ומים.
Yesh li yayin adom, yayin lavan, mits tapoozeem vemayim.
I've got red wine, white wine, orange juice and water.

מאוד שמחתי שבאת!
Me'od samakhti shebat (fem.) / shebata (masc.).
Thanks so much for coming. I'm glad you could come.

סע / סעי בזהירות!
Sa (masc.) / Se'ee (fem.) bezeheeroot!
Drive carefully!

את רוצה / אתה רוצה לישון פה?
At rotza (fem.) / Ata rotzeh (masc.) lishon po?
Would you like to stay the night?

אראה לך את החדר.
Ar'eh lakh (fem.) / lekha (masc.) et hakheder.
I'll show you your room.

תגידי / תגיד לי אם את צריכה / אתה צריך משהו.
Tageedi (fem.) / Tageed (masc.) lee im at tsreekha (fem.) / ata tsareekh (masc.) mashehu.
Tell me if you need anything.

לילה טוב, תישני / תישן טוב.
Layla tov, tishnee (fem.) / tishan (masc.) tov!
Good night, sleep well!

ישנת טוב?
Yashant (fem.) / Yashanta (masc.) tov?
Did you sleep well?

ארוחת הבוקר מוכנה!
Arookhat haboker mookhana!
Breakfast is ready!

1.3 SMALL TALK

?מאיפה את / אתה
Me'eyfo at (fem.) / ata (masc.)?
Where do you come from?

אני מתל אביב. ואת? ואתה?
Anee miTel Aviv. Ve'at (fem.) /Ve'ata (masc.)?
I come from Tel Aviv. And you?

?במה את עוסקת / אתה עוסק
Bemah at osseket (fem.) / ata ossek (masc.)?
What do you do for a living?

אני עורך דין בסימנס.
Anee orekh deen beSiemens.
I work as a lawyer for Siemens.

אני כרגע מובטלת / מובטל.
Anee karega muvtelet (fem.) / muvtal (masc.).
I'm currently unemployed.

אני סטודנט. אני סטודנטית.
Anee student. Anee studentit.
I'm a student (male/female).

?מה את לומדת? מה אתה לומד
Ma at lomedet (fem.)? Ma ata lomed (masc.)?
What do you study?

אני לומדת / לומד תואר שני במנהל עסקים.
Anee lomedet (fem.) / lomed (masc.) toar shenee beminhal
assakeem.
I'm getting my master's in business administration.

האוכל פה מצוין.
Ha'okhel po metsuyan.
The food here is delicious.

את רוצה / אתה רוצה לשתות עוד משהו?
At rotsa (fem.) / Ata rotseh lishtot od mashehu?
Would you like to have another drink?

אני לא יכול / יכולה לשתות, אני נוהג / נוהגת.
Anee lo yakhol (masc.) / yekholah (fem.) lishtot, anee noheg (masc.)
/ noheget (fem.).
I can't drink, I'm driving.

אני חייבת / חייב ללכת.
Anee khayevet (fem.) / khayav (masc.) lalekhet.
I need to go.

אולי ניפגש מתישהו.
Oolay neepagesh matayshehoo.
Maybe we can meet some time.

כן, בכיף. הנה המספר שלי.
Ken, bekef. Heene hamispar sheli.
Yes, that would be nice. Here is my phone number.

אני גם בפייסבוק. השם שלי אבי כהן.
Anee gam beFacebook. Hashem sheli Avi Cohen.
I'm also on Facebook. My name is Avi Cohen.

מאוד נהניתי לדבר איתך.
Me'od neheneti ledaber itakh (fem.) / itkha (masc.).
It was really nice talking to you.

נתראה אחר כך.
Nitra'eh akhar kakh.
See you later.

שיהיה לך ערב נעים!
She'ihye lakh (fem.) / lekha (masc.) erev na'eem!
Have a nice rest of the evening!

1.4 TALKING ABOUT YOURSELF

אני מארצות הברית.
Anee meArtsot HaBrit.
I'm from the United States.

אני גר/ה שנה בתל אביב.
Ani gar (masc.) / gara (fem.) shana beTel Aviv.
I've lived in Tel Aviv for a year.

אני שוכר/ת דירה בצפון הישן.
Anee ssokher (masc.) / ssokheret (fem.) deerah batsafon hayashan.
I rent an apartment in the Old North.

אני גר/ה עם שותף.
Anee gar (masc.) / gara (fem.) eem shootaf.
I have a roommate.

אני נשוי / נשואה פלוס 2.
Anee nasuy (masc.) / nesua (fem.) plus shtayim.
I'm married and I have two children.

אני גרוש/ה - רווק/ה.
Anee garoosh (masc.) / groosha (fem.) – ravak (masc.) / ravaka (fem.).
I'm divorced - single.

יש לי חבר/ה.
Yesh lee khaver / khavera.
I have a boyfriend / a girlfriend.

יש לי אחות / אח.
Yesh lee akhot / akh.
I have a sister / a brother.

אין לי אחים ואחיות.
Eyn lee akhim ve'akhayot.
I don't have siblings.

ההורים שלי גרים באוסטרליה.
HaHoreem shelee gareem be'Ostralia.
My parents live in Australia.

למדתי רפואה בניו יורק.
Lamadeti refu'a beNew York.
I studied medicine in New York.

יש לי תואר שני במדעי המחשב.
Yesh li to'ar shenee be'mada'ey hamakhshev.
I have a Master's degree in computer science.

אני מתכנת בחברת סטארט אפ.
Anee metakhnet bekhevrat start-up.
I work as a developer for a start-up company.

אני זמר/ת – מוסיקאי/ת – אמן/ית – רקדן/ית
Anee zamar/zameret – musikay/musika'it – oman/omanit - rakdan/rakdanit.
I'm a singer / musician / artist / dancer.

אני מחפש/ת עבודה.
Anee mekhapes (masc.) mekhapeset (fem.) avodah.
I'm looking for a job.

אישתי עובדת חצי משרה.
Ishtee ovedet khatzee misrah.
My wife works part-time.

1.5 TELLING STORIES

סיפרתי לך כבר מה קרה?
Siparti lekha (masc.) / lakh (fem.) kvar mah karah?
Have I told you what happened?

אתה לא תאמין מה קרה לי.
Ata lo ta'ameen ma karah lee.
You won't believe what happened to me.

היית צריך לראות את זה.
Hayita tzarikh lir'ot et ze.
You should have seen that.

הייתי בדרך לעבודה.
Hayiti baderekh la'avodah.
I was on my way to work.

הייתי בדרך חזרה מבפאב.
Hayiti baderekh khazarah meha"pub".
I was on my way back from the pub.

שמתי לב ש...
Samti lev she...
I noticed that...

ואז אמרה האישה:
Ve'az amrah ha'ishah:
Then the woman said...

ומסיבה כלשהי...
Vemisiba kolshehee...
And for whatever reason...

ובדיוק ברגע הזה התחיל לרדת גשם.
Vebediuk barega hazeh hitkheel laredet geshem.
In that very moment it started raining.

ופתאום היא עמדה לידי.
Vepit'om hee amdah leyadee.
And suddenly she stood next to me.

ואז אמרתי:
Ve'az amarti:
Then I said:

אתה קולט?
Ata kolet?
Can you imagine that?

חשבתי שזה מוזר.
Khashavti she'zeh moozar.
I was thinking to myself that this was strange.

ואז, אחרי שהיא הלכה,...
Ve'az, akhrey she'hee halkhah,...
And then, after she was gone, ...

לא הצלחתי להאמין.
Lo hetzlakhi leha'ameen.
I could hardly believe it.

הייתי כל כך שמח/שמחה.
Hayiti kol kakh same'akh (masc.) / smekhah (fem.).
I was so happy about it.

אתה מתאר לעצמך איך הרגשתי?
Ata meta'er le'atzmekha (masc.) / le'atzmekh (fem.) eykh hirgashti?
Can you imagine how I felt?

ודרך אגב,...

Vederekh agav,...

And by the way, ...

למזלי היה לי את הפלאפון.

Lemazali haya li et hapelefon.

Luckily I had my cell phone with me.

הכל קרה כל כך מהר.

Hakol karah kol kakh maher.

It all happened so fast.

כמעט שכחתי לציין ש...

Kim'at shakhakhti letzayen she...

I totally forgot to mention that...

ברור שלא יכולתי לדעת ש...

Barur she'lo yakholti lada'at she...

Of course I couldn't have known that...

טוב, בסוף הלכנו הביתה.

Tov, basof halakhnu habayta.

So eventually we went home.

היה כמו בסרט.

Haya kmo be'seret.

It was like in a movie.

1.6 BOOKS, MOVIES & MUSIC

אני אוהב לקרוא ספרים.

Anee ohev likro sfarim.

I like reading books.

אני קורא כרגע ספר לימוד על פסיכולוגיה.
Anee koreh karega sefer limud al psikhologia.
I'm currently reading a textbook about psychology.

אני לא אוהב ספרי מדע בדיוני.
Anee lo ohev sifrey mada bidyonee.
I don't like science fiction books.

אתה אוהב לקרוא? את אוהבת לקרוא?
Ata ohev likro? (masc.) At ohevet likro? (fem.)
Do you like reading?

אהבת את הספר האחרון של דן בראון?
Ahavta (masc.) / Ahavt (fem.) et hasefer ha'akharon shel Dan Brown?
Did you like Dan Brown's last book?

הספר היה טוב, אבל הסוף היה מאכזב.
Hasefer haya tov, aval hasof haya me'akhzev.
The book was very good, but the end disappointed me.

היה מאוד מותח.
Haya me'od mote'akh.
It was very exciting.

אני אוהב לראות סרטי אימה /ָ קומדיות / סרטי פעולה.
Anee ohev lir'ot sirtey eymah / komediot / sirtey pe'oolah.
I like watching horror movies / comedies / action movies.

מה אתה אוהב לראות? מה את אוהבת לראות?
Ma ata ohev lir'ot? (masc.) Ma at ohevet lir'ot? (fem.)
What do you like watching?

ראיתי את הבקרוב.
Ra'iti et habekarov.
I saw the trailer.

הספר יותר טוב מהסרט.
Hasefer yoter tov mehaseret.
The book is better than the movie.

ראיתי את הסרט בקולנוע.
Ra'iti et haseret bakolno'a.
I saw the film at the theater.

אני מחכה עד שייצא הדי.וי.די.
Ani mekhakeh ad she'yetzeh ha-DVD.
I'll wait for the DVD to be released.

הורדתי אותו באינטרנט.
Horadeti oto ba'internet.
I downloaded it from the internet.

לדעתי הסרט מעולה.
Leda'ati haseret me'ooleh.
I think the movie is awesome.

אני לא יכול / יכולה לחיות בלי מוסיקה.
Anee lo yakhol (masc.) / yekholah (fem.) likhyot blee moozikah.
I can't live without music.

תמיד יש איתי נגן אם פי 3.
Tamid yesh iti nagan MP3.
I always carry my mp3-player with me.

איזה מוסיקה אתה אוהב לשמוע?
Eyzeh moozikah ata ohev lishmo'a?
What kind of music do you like?

אתה אוהב רוק / פופ / ג'אז?
Ata ohev rock / pop / jazz?
Do you like rock / pop / jazz music?

אני אוהב מוסיקה קלאסית.
Anee ohev moozikah klassit.
I love classical music.

קניתי את הדיסק החדש של שלמה ארצי.
Kaneeti et hadisk hakhadash shel Shlomo Artzi.
I bought Shlomo Artzi's new CD.

אני לא מת על הבי מטאל.
Anee lo met al heavy metal.
I'm not a huge Heavy Metal fan.

בדרך כלל אני שומע רדיו.
Bederekh klal anee shome'a radio.
Usually I listen to the radio.

1.7 TALKING ABOUT SOCCER / FOOTBALL

אני אוהב לשחק כדורגל. אני אוהב לראות כדורגל.
Anee ohev lesakhek kaduregel. Anee ohev lir'ot kaduregel.
I like playing soccer. I like watching soccer.

הקבוצה האהובה עליי היא מכבי תל אביב.
Hakvootzah ha'ahoovah alai hee Maccabi Tel Aviv.
My favorite team is Maccabi Tel Aviv.

השחקן האהוב עליי הוא אבי כהן.
Hassakhkan ha'ahoov alai hoo Avi Cohen.
My favorite player is Avi Cohen.

הוא שוער.
Hoo sho'er.
He's a goalkeeper.

כמה כמה? שתיים אפס.
Kama kama? Shtayim efes.
What's the score? It's 2 to 0.

מכבי מובילה שלוש אחת.
Maccabi movilah shalosh akhat.
Maccabi leads by a score of 3 to 1.

תיקו.
Teko.
The game is tied.

זה היה גול עצמי.
Ze haya gol atzmee.
That was an own goal.

החלוץ הבקיע שער במחצית הראשונה (השנייה).
HaKhaluts hivkeea sha'ar bamakhatseet harishonah (hashniyyah).
The forward scored a goal in the first (second) half.

השופט נתן בעיטת עונשין (פנדל).
Hashofet natan be'itat onsheen (pendel).
The referee called a penalty.

הבלם קיבל כרטיס צהוב.
Habalam kibel kartis tsahov.
The defender got a yellow card.

הקשר קיבל כרטיס אדום.
Hakashar kibel kartis adom.
The midfielder got a red card.

אחרי הפסקת המחצית החליף המאמן את הקפטן.
Akhrey hafsakat hamakhatsit hekhlif hame'amen et hakepten.
After half-time, the coach substituted out the captain.

הקווו מצביע על נבדל.
Hakavan matsbee'a al nivdal.
The linesman called offside.

החלוץ נמצא בנבדל.
HaKhaluts nimtsah benivdal.
The forward is offside.

זאת הייתה עבירה קשה.
Zot haytah averah kashah.
That was a bad foul.

הפועל מקבלת כדור חופשי.
Hapo'el mekabelet kadoor khofshi.
Hapo'el gets a free kick.

הייתה הארכה של שלוש דקות.
Haytah ha'arakhah shel shalosh dakot.
There was an extra time of 3 minutes.

מי ניצח?
Mee nitse'akh?
Who won?

איך נגמר המשחק?
Eykh nigmar hamiskhak?
How did the game end?

מכבי ניצחה ארבע שלוש.
Maccabi nitzkhah arba shalosh.
Maccabi won 4 to 3.

הפועל הפסידה שתיים אפס.
Hapo'el hifsida shtayim efes.
Hapo'el lost 0 to 2.

SECTION 2: SHOPPING, FOOD & SERVICES

2.1 BUYING CLOTHES AND SHOES

אני רק מסתכל, תודה.
Anee rak mistakel, todah.
I'm just looking around, thank you.

אני רוצה את החולצה מחלון הראווה.
Anee rotseh et hakhultzah mikhalon hara'avah.
I would like to have the shirt from the shop window.

יש לך את החולצה ב - XL / L / M / S
Yesh lekha et hakhultsah be- S / M / L / XL?
Do you have the shirt in S / M / L / XL?

יש לך את המכנסיים מידה אחת יותר גדולה / קטנה?
Yesh lekha et hamikhnassayim midah akhat yoter gdolah / ktanah?
Do you have the pants one size larger / smaller?

אני יכול למדוד את החולצה השחורה?
Anee yakhol limdod et hakhultsah hashkhorah?
Can I try on the black shirt?

יש לך את החולצה גם בכחול?
Yesh lekha et hakhultsah gam bekakhol?
Do you also have the shirt in blue?

סליחה, איפה תאי המדידה?
Slikhah, eyfo ta'ey hamedida?
Excuse me, where are the fitting rooms?

מה אתה חושב? המעיל מתאים לי?
Ma atah khoshev? Hame'eel mat'eem lee?
What do you think? Does the coat look good on me?

הנעליים האלה גם במבצע?
Hana'alayim ha'ele gam bemivtsah?
Are these shoes also on sale?

המידה שלי 42.
Hameedah sheli 42.
I wear size 42.

הנעליים קטנות / גדולות מדי.
Hana'alayim ktanot / gdolot miday.
The shoes are too small / too big.

הנעל השמאלית לוחצת.
Hana'al hasmalit lokhetset.
The left shoe pinches.

אני לוקח את החולצה ואת הנעליים החומות.
Anee loke'akh et hakhultsah ve'et hana'alayim hakhumot.
I'll take the shirt and the brown shoes.

אני רוצה להחליף את החולצה.
Anee rotsah lehakhleef et hasimlah.
I'd like to exchange the dress.

כמה זה עולה? אפשר לשלם בכרטיס אשראי?
Kama ze oleh? Efshar leshalem bekartis ashray?
How much is that? Can I pay by credit card?

איפה הקופה?
Eyfo hakupah?
Where's the checkout counter?

2.2 AT THE RESTAURANT

שולחן לשניים, בבקשה.
Shulkhan leshnayim bevakashah.
A table for 2, please.

יש איזור ללא מעשנים?
Yesh eyzor lelo me'ashneem?
Is there a non-smoking area?

איפה אני יכול לשטוף ידיים?
Eyfo anee yakhol lishtof yadayim?
Where can I wash my hands?

אני רוצה את התפריט בבקשה.
Anee rotseh et hatafrit bevakashah.
I'd like to have the menu.

יש תפריט באנגלית?
Yesh tafrit be'anglit?
Do you have a menu in English?

יש מנות צמחוניות?
Yesh manot tsimkhoniyot?
Do you also have vegetarian dishes?

יש מנות בלי גלוטן?
Yesh manot bli gluten?
Are there gluten free dishes?

אני אלרגי לאגוזים.
Anee alergi le'egozeem.
I'm allergic to nuts.

אני רוצה להזמין.
Anee rotseh lehazmeen.
I'd like to order.

אני רוצה את המרק כמנה ראשונה ואת הלזניה כמנה עיקרית.
Anee rotseh et hamarak kemanah rishonah ve'et halazania
kemanah ikareet.
*I'd like to have the soup as an appetizer and the lasagna as my main
course.*

אפשר כוס מים?
Efshar kos mayim?
Can I have a glass of water?

אתה יכול להביא לי מזלג? כף - סכין
Ata yakhol lehavee lee mazleg? - kaf -sakeen
Could you bring me a fork, please? – a spoon – a knife

איזה קינוחים יש?
Eyze kinookheem yesh?
What desserts do you have?

היה טעים מאוד, תודה רבה.
Haya ta'eem me'od, todah rabah.
It was delicious, thank you.

האוכל היה מעולה.
Ha'okhel haya me'ooleh.
The food was delicious.

אפשר עוד מפית?
Efshar od mapit?
Can I have another napkin?

אני רוצה לשלם.
Anee rotseh leshalem.
I'd like to pay.

חשבון בבקשה.
Kheshbon bevakashah.
The bill / check please.

אפשר לשלם בכרטיס אשראי?
Efshar leshalem bekartis ashray?
Can I pay by credit card?

תשמור את העודף.
Tishmor et ha'odef.
Keep the change.

סליחה, איפה השירותים?
Slikhah, eyfo hasherooteem?
Excuse me, where is the bathroom?

2.3 BUYING A CELL PHONE SIM CARD

אני רוצה לקנות כרטיס סים לטלפון הנייד שלי.
Anee rotseh liknot kartis SIM latelefon hanayad sheli.
I'd like to buy a SIM card for my cell phone.

אני רוצה כרטיס סים בתשלום מראש.
Anee rotseh kartis SIM betashloom merosh.
I'd like a prepaid SIM card.

אני רוצה חבילת סלולר.
Anee rotseh khavilat selular.
I'd like to have a contract for my cell phone.

מה המספר החדש שלי?
Ma hamispar hakhadash shelee?
What's my new cell phone number?

כמה דקות כלולות בחבילה?
Kama dakot klulot bakhaveelah?
How many minutes are included in the plan?

כמה הודעות אס. אם. אס. אפשר לשלוח בחודש?
Kama hoda'ot SMS efshar lishlo'akh bekhodesh?
How many texts can I send per month?

מה הגודל של חבילת הגלישה?
Ma hagodel shel khavilat haglisha?
How much data is included?

כמה עולה דקת שיחה?
Kama olah dakat sikhah?
What's the cost per minute?

אני רוצה חבילה שכוללת שיחות והודעות ללא הגבלה.
Anee rotseh khaveelah shekolelet sikhot vehoda'ot lelo hagbalah.
I'd like an unlimited talk & text plan.

איפה אני יכול להטעין את החשבון פרי פייד?
Eyfo anee yakhol lehat'een et kheshbon hapripeyd? ("pre-paid")
Where can I add credit to my cell phone?

עד מתי הכרטיס בתוקף?
Ad matay hakartis betokef?
How long is the SIM card valid?

הכרטיס עובד גם בחו"ל?
Hakartis oved gam bekhool?
Does the card also work abroad?

אני צריך מיקרו סים (נאנו סים).
Anee tsarikh micro-SIM (nano-SIM).
I need a micro SIM (nano SIM).

הכרטיס כולל סכום התחלתי?
Hakartis kolel skhum hatkhalati?
Is there an initial balance in my card?

יש התחייבות?

Yesh hitkhayvut?

Are there any contract obligations?

אני יכול להוסיף חבילת גלישה?

Anee yakhol lehoseef khavilat glishah?

Can I add a data plan?

2.4 AT THE POST OFFICE

אני רוצה לאסוף חבילה.

Anee rotseh le'esof khavilah.

I'd like to pick up a package.

כמה עולה בול לקנדה?

Kama oleh bool leKanada?

How much is a stamp to Canada?

אני רוצה לשלוח את הגלויה הזאת בדואר אוויר.

Anee rotseh lishloakh et haglooyah hazot bedo'ar aveer.

I'd like to send this post card by air mail.

אני רוצה לשלוח את המכתב הזה בדואר רשום.

Anee rotseh lishloakh et hamikhtav hazeh bedo'ar rashoom.

I'd like to send this letter by registered mail.

אני רוצה לשלוח את החבילה הזאת לברזיל.

Anee rotseh lishloakh et hakhavilah hazot leBrazil.

I'd like to send this package to Brazil.

איפה יש פה תיבת דואר?

Eyfo yesh po teyvat hado'ar?

Where's the nearest mailbox?

אתם מוכרים מעטפות מבוילות?
Atem mokhrim ma'atafot mevuyalot?
Do you sell prepaid envelopes?

התוכן שביר.
Hatokhen shaveer.
The content is fragile.

2.5 AT THE BANK

אני רוצה למשוך 50 שקלים.
Anee rotseh limshokh khameesheem shkaleem.
I'd like to withdraw 50 Shekels.

אני רוצה להפקיד 50 שקלים.
Anee rotseh lehafkeed khameesheem shkaleem.
I'd like to deposit 50 Shekels.

איפה יש פה כספומט?
Eyfo yesh po kaspomat?
Where's the nearest ATM?

אני רוצה לפתוח חשבון.
Anee rotseh liftoakh kheshbon.
I'd like to open a bank account.

אני צריך חשבון עובר ושב וחשבון חיסכון.
Anee tsarikh kheshbon over vashav vekheshbon khisakhon.
I need a checking account and a savings account.

מה גובה העמלות?
Ma gova ha'amlot?
How much are the fees?

אני מקבל גם כרטיס אשראי?
Anee mekabel gam kartis ashray?
Do I also get a credit card?

אני יכול למשוך כסף בחו"ל עם הכרטיס הזה?
Ani yakhol limshokh kesef bekhool eem hakartis hazeh?
Can I use the card to withdraw money abroad?

כמה מסגרת האשראי?
Kama misgeret ha'ashray?
What's the credit card limit?

אני רוצה לעשות העברה.
Anee rotseh la'asot ha'avarah.
I'd like to make a bank transfer.

אני רוצה להעביר 1000 שקל מהחשבון עובר ושב לחשבון חיסכון.
Anee rotseh leha'aveer elef shekel mehakheshon over vashav
lakheshbon khisakhon.
*I'd like to transfer 1000 shekels from my current account to my
savings account.*

אני יכול לעשות את זה באינטרנט?
Anee yakhol la'asot et zeh bainternet?
Can I use online banking for this?

אני רוצה להמיר דולר לשקלים.
Anee rotseh lehamir dollar leshkaleem.
I'd like to change Dollars into Shekels.

יש לך שטרות של מאה?
Yesh lekha shtarot shel me'a?
Do you have 100 shekel bills?

אני רוצה להפקיד את הצ'ק הזה.
Anee rotzeh lehafkid et hacheck hazeh.
I'd like to cash this check.

ATM INSTRUCTIONS

הכנס את כרטיסך.
Please insert your card.

הכנס את הקוד הסודי.
Please enter your PIN.

בחר את הסכום המבוקש.
Please choose the desired amount.

לאישור לחץ על המקש הירוק.
Please press the green button to confirm.

בקשתך בטיפול.
Your request is being processed.

הוצא את כרטיסך.
Please take your card.

הוצא את כספך.
Please take your money.

2.6 LOOKING FOR AN APARTMENT

ראיתי את המודעה שלך באינטרנט.
Ra'eeti et hamoda'ah shelkha ba'internet.
I saw your ad on the internet.

אני מעוניין בדירה.
Anee me'unyan badirah.
I'm interested in the apartment.

הדירה עדיין פנויה?
Hadirah adayin pnooyah?
Is the apartment still available?

מה שכר הדירה?
Ma skhar hadirah?
How much is the rent?

כמה החשבונות?
Kama hakheshbonot?
How much are the utilities?

החשבונות כלולים בשכר הדירה?
Hakheshbonot klulim beskhar hadira?
Are the utilities included in the rent?

מה גובה הפיקדון?
Ma gova hapikadon?
How much is the deposit?

כמה חדרים יש בדירה?
Kama khadareem yesh badeera?
How many rooms does the apartment have?

הדירה מרוהטת או לא?
Hadeera meroohetet o lo?
Is the apartment furnished or unfurnished?

ממתי הדירה פנויה?
Mimatay hadeerah pnooyah?
When is the apartment available?

מתי אפשר לעבור?
Matay efshar la'avor?
When could I move in?

זו דירה עם שותפים?
Zo deerah eem shootafeem?
Is it a room share?

כמה שותפים יש?
Kama shootafeem yesh?
How many roommates are there?

הבניין ישן או חדש?
Habinyan yashan o khadash?
Is it an old building or a new building?

הדירה משופצת?
Hadeerah meshoopetzet?
Is the apartment renovated?

יש מרפסת בדירה?
Yesh mirpeset badeerah?
Does the apartment have a balcony?

באיזו קומה נמצאת הדירה?
Be'eyzo komah nimetzet hadeerah?
What floor is the apartment on?

מתי אפשר לראות אותה?
Matay efshar lir'ot otah?
When can I have a look at it (the apartment)?

איפה בדיוק נמצאת הדירה?
Eyfo bediyook nimtzet hadeerah?
Where is the apartment located exactly?

באיזו שכונה זה?
Be'eyzo shkhoonah zeh?
What neighborhood is that?

מה הכתובת המדוייקת, בבקשה?
Ma haktovet hamedooyeket, bėvakashah?
What is the exact address please?

יש תחנת אוטובוס בסביבה?
Yesh takhanat otoboos basveevah?
Is there a bus station nearby?

האיזור בטוח?
Ha'eyzor batoo'akh?
Is the area safe?

2.7 USING TAXIS AND PUBLIC TRANSPORTATION

אני רוצה לקנות כרטיס לתל אביב.
Anee rotseh liknot kartis leTel Aviv.
I'd like to buy a ticket to Tel Aviv.

כמה עולה כרטיס יומי?
Kama oleh kartis yomi?
How much is a day ticket?

יש הנחה לסטודנטים?
Yesh hanakhah lestoodenteem?
Is there a discount for students?

אני רוצה חופשי חודשי.
Anee rotseh khofshee khodshee.
I'd like a monthly ticket.

איזה קו מגיע לכותל?
Eyze kav megee'a laKotel?
Which bus goes to the Wailing Wall?

איפה יש פה תחנת אוטובוס?
Eyfo yesh po takhanat otoboos?
Where is the nearest bus stop?

איפה יש פה תחנת רכבת?
Eyfo yesh po takhanat rakevet?
Is there a train station around here?

לאיזה כיוון אני צריך לנסוע?
Le'eyzeh kivoon anee tsareekh linso'a?
In which direction do I need to go?

איפה אני צריך לרדת?
Eyfo anee tsareekh laredet?
Where do I have to get off?

אפשר לקבל לוח זמנים?
Efshar lekabel looakh zmaneem?
Can I have a time-table please?

איזה קו מגיע לתחנה המרכזית?
Eyze kav megee'a latakhanah hamerkazeet?
Which line gets me to the central bus station?

איפה יש פה מכונת כרטיסים?
Eyfo yesh po mekhonat kartiseem?
Where's the ticket machine?

מתי מגיעה הרכבת הבאה?
Matay megee'ah harakevet haba'ah?
When does the next train arrive?

הרכבת הזאת נוסעת לשדה התעופה?
Harakevet hazot nosa'at lesdeh hate'oofah?
Does this train go to the airport?

אני צריך להחליף אוטובוס בירושלים?
Anee tsareekh lahakhleef otoboos birooshalayeem?
Do I need to change buses in Jerusalem?

כמה תחנות זה?
Kama takhanot zeh?
How many stops is it?

הולכים ברגל או שניקח מונית?
Holkheem baregel o shenikakh moneet?
Do we walk or should we take a taxi?

תוכל להזמין לי מונית בבקשה?
Tukhal lehazmeen lee moneet bevakashah?
Could you call me a taxi, please?

אתה פנוי?
Ata panooy?
Are you available?

אתה יכול להפעיל את המונה בבקשה?
Ata yakhol lehaf'eel et hamoneh bevakashah?
Could you turn on the taximeter, please?

כמה זה עולה לשדה התעופה?
Kama ze oleh lesdeh hate'oofah?
How much is it to the airport?

לרחוב בן יהודה 55 בבקשה.
Lirkhov ben yehooda 55 bevakashah.
To 55 Ben Yehuda street, please.

אתה יכול לעצור פה.
Ata yakhol la'atsor po.
You can stop here.

תשמור את העודף.
Tishmor et ha'odef.
Keep the change.

SECTION 3: SPEAKING ON THE PHONE

3.1 USEFUL EXPRESSIONS FOR PHONE CALLS

?הלו
Hallo?
Hello?

?שלום, מדבר יוסי. אפרת נמצאת
Shalom, medaber Yossi. Efrat nimtzet?
Hi, this is Yossi. Is Efrat home?

?קיבלת את ההודעה שלי
Kibalta et hahoda'ah shelee?
Did you get my message?

.היה תפוס
Haya tafoos.
The line was busy.

.הגעתי למענה הקולי
Higatee lama'aneh hakolee.
The voicemail answered.

!כיף שהתקשרת
Kef shehitkasharta.
I appreciate your call!

.רק רגע בבקשה, מישהו נמצא בקו השני
Rak rega bevakashah, mishehoo nimtzah bakav hashenee.
One moment, please. There is someone on the other line.

אני יכול לחזור אליך?
Anee yakhol lakhzor eleykha?
Can I call you back?

השיחה התנתקה.
Hasikhah hitnatkah.
The line was cut off.

אני בקושי שומע אותך.
Anee bekoshi shome'a otkhah.
I can hardly hear you.

אני רוצה להשאיר הודעה.
Anee rotseh lehash'eer hoda'ah.
I'd like to leave a message.

אני יכול למסור משהו?
Anee yakhol limsor mashehoo?
Can I take a message?

אתה יכול להגיד לו בבקשה שיחזור אליי?
Ata yakhol lehageed lo bevakashah sheyakhzor elay?
Can you please tell him to call me back?

הוא ניתק באמצע השיחה.
Hoo nitek be'emtza haseekhah.
He hung up on me.

3.2 BUSINESS PHONE CALLS

איך אפשר לעזור?
Eykh efshar la'azor?
How may I help you?

שלום, שמי דויד כהן.

Shalom. Shmee David Cohen.

Good afternoon. This is David Cohen.

סליחה, טעות במספר.

Slikhah, ta'oot bamispar.

Excuse me, I've dialed the wrong number.

אפשר לדבר עם דנה לוי מהמכירות?

Efshar ledaber eem Dana Levy mehamekheerot?

Can I speak to Dana Levy from sales?

במה מדובר?

Bameh medoobar?

Can I ask what it's about?

רק רגע, אני מעביר את השיחה.

Rak rega, anee ma'aveer et haseekhah.

One moment please, I'll put you through.

אני מנסה להעביר אותך.

Anee menaseh leha'aveer otkhah.

I'll try to connect you.

אל תנתק.

Al tenatek.

Please hold.

השלוחה שלה 123.

Hashlookhah shelah 123.

Her extension is 123.

לא עונים.
Lo oneem.
I'm afraid there is no answer.

הקו תפוס. אתה רוצה להמתין?
Hakav tafoos. Ata rotseh lehamteen?
The line is busy. Would you like to hold?

אנסה שוב יותר מאוחר.
Anaseh shoov yoter me'ookhar.
I'll try again later.

אפשר לחזור אליך?
Efshar lakhzor eleykha?
Can we call you back?

תודה רבה, אבל אני אנסה שוב יותר מאוחר.
Todah rabah, aval anee anaseh shoov yoter me'ookhar.
It's alright, thank you. I'll call back later.

אשים לה את ההודעה על השולחן.
Asim lah et hahoda'ah al hashoolkhan.
I'll put the message on her desk.

מר גולדמן נמצא בישיבה.
Mar Goldman nimtza beyeshiva.
Mr Goldman is in a meeting.

אתה יודע מתי הוא יחזור?
Ata yode'a matay hoo yakhzor?
Do you know when he'll be back?

אולי תוכל לעזור לי.

Oolay tukhal la'azor lee.

Maybe you can help me?

מדובר ב...

Medoobar be...

I'm calling about...

מאיפה אתה מתקשר?

Mi'eyfo ata mitkasher?

Where are you calling from, please?

איך? אתה יכול לאיית את זה?

Eykh? Ata yakhol le'ayet et zeh?

Excuse me? Could you spell that, please?

תודה שהתקשרת.

Todah shehitkasharta.

Thank you for calling.

להתראות.

Lehitra'ot.

Goodbye!

3.3 TALKING ON THE CELL PHONE

אתה יכול להשיג אותי בנייד.

Ata yakhol lehaseeg oti banayad.

You can reach me on my cell phone.

הנייד שלו לא דלוק.
Hanayad shelo lo dalook.
His cell phone is not switched on.

שלחתי לה הודעה.
Shalakhti la hoda'ah.
I sent her a text.

הסוללה שלי נגמרת עוד מעט, אתקשר אליך יותר מאוחר.
Hasolelah shelee nigmeret od me'at, etkasher eleykha yoter me'ookhar.
My battery is about to die, I'll call you back later.

השיחה תיכף תתנתק, אני במעלית.
Hasikha tekhef titnatek, ani bema'aleet.
I'm going to lose you in a moment, I'm inside an elevator.

אין לי קליטה. הקליטה גרועה.
Eyn lee klitah. Hakleetah gru'ah.
I don't have any reception. I have bad reception.

אני רוצה לקנות דיבורית לרכב.
Anee rotseh liknot dibooreet larekhev.
I'd like to buy a hands free device for the car.

תתקשר אליי לקו הנייח, בבקשה.
Titkasher elay lakav hanayakh, bevakashah.
Please call me on my landline.

3.4 ORDERING TAKE-OUT

שלום, אני רוצה להזמין פיצה.
Shalom, anee rotseh lehazmeen Pizza.
Hi, I'd like to order a pizza.

אני רוצה את הפיצה עם פפרוני ופטריות.
Anee rotseh et hapizza eem peperoni vepitriyot.
I'd like the pizza with pepperoni and mushrooms.

אני רוצה גם בקבוק ליטר וחצי של קולה.
Anee rotseh gam bakbook liter vakhetsi shel cola.
I'd also like a 1.5 Liter bottle of coke.

אני רוצה להזמין מספר 23 ומספר 16.
Anee rotseh lehazmeen mispar 23 vemispar 16.
I'd like to order #23 and #16.

מה אתה ממליץ?
Mah ata mamleets?
What do you recommend?

הכתובת שלי היא רחוב בן יהודה מספר 5 קומה שנייה.
Haktovet shelee hee rekhov ben yehooda mispar 5 komah shniyah.
My address is 5 Ben Yehuda Street, second floor.

מספר הטלפון שלי הוא 8562345.
Mispar hatelefon shelee hoo 856 23 45.
My phone number is 856 23 45.

אתה יכול לדבר יותר לעט בבקשה?
Ata yakhol ledaber yoter le'at bevakashah?
Can you speak more slowly, please?

אתה יכול לחזור על זה בבקשה?
Ata yakhol lakhzor al zeh bevakashah?
Could you repeat that, please?

אתה רוצה מרק או קינוח?
Ata rotseh marak o kinoo'akh?
Would you like to order a soup or a dessert?

לא תודה, זה הכל.
Lo todah, zeh hakol.
No thanks, that's all.

כמה זמן לוקח המשלוח?
Kamah zman loke'akh hamishlo'akh?
How long does delivery take?

מתי אני יכול לבוא לאסוף את ההזמנה?
Matay anee yakhol lavo le'esof et hahazmanah?
When can I pick up my order?

אני יכול לשלם במזומן?
Anee yakhol leshalem bemezooman?
Can I pay cash?

תודה רבה, להתראות.
Todah rabah, lehitra'ot.
Thanks a lot, good bye!

3.5 RESERVING A TABLE

אני רוצה להזמין שולחן להיום בערב.
Anee rotseh lehazmeen shulkhan lehayom ba'erev.
I'd like to reserve a table for tonight.

לאיזו שעה?
Le'eyzo sha'ah?
For what time?

ל-19:30 בבקשה. (שבע וחצי)
Le-19:30 bevakashah (sheva vakhetsi).
At 7:30pm.

לכמה אנשים?
Lekama anasheem?
For how many people?

אנחנו קבוצה של ארבעה.
Anakhnoo kvootsah shel arba'ah.
We're a group of 4.

אתם רוצים לשבת בפנים או בחוץ?
Atem rotseem lashevet bifneem o bakhoots?
Would you like to be seated inside or outside?

בפנים בבקשה, אם אפשר ליד החלון.
Bifneem bevakashah. Eem efshar leyad hakhalon.
Inside, please. If possible, next to the window.

יש איזור ללא מעשנים?
Yesh eyzor lelo me'ashneem?
Is there a non-smoking area?

על איזה שם אני אשמור את השולחן?
Al eyze shem ani eshmor et hashulkhan?
To what name should I reserve the table?

מה שמך בבקשה?
Mah shimkhah bevakashah?
What's your name, please?

אני מצטער אבל אנחנו כבר מלאים.
Anee mitsta'er, aval anakhnoo kvar mele'eem.
I'm sorry, but we're fully booked.

יש לנו שולחן בשעה שמונה. זה מתאים לכם?
Yesh lanoo shulkhan besha'ah shmoneh. Ze mat'eem lakhem?
We have a table at 8pm. Does that work for you?

כן זה מתאים.
Ken, zeh mat'eem.
Yes, that works for me.

מה מספר הטלפון שלך?
Mah mispar hatelefon shelkha?
What's your phone number?

מספר הטלפון שלי הוא 4561234.
Mispar hatelefon shelee hoo 456123.
My phone number is 456 12 34.

תודה רבה, להתראות.
Todah rabah, lehitra'ot.
Thank you very much. See you later.

3.6 MAKING APPOINTMENTS

אהלן, אני עושה מסיבה אצלי בבית בשבת.
Ahlan, ani oseh mesibah etzlee babayit beshabat.
Hi, I'm throwing a party at my place on Saturday.

בא לך לבוא?
Ba lekha lavo?
Are you coming along?

אשמח אם תוכל לבוא.
Esmakh eem tookhal lavo.
I'd love it if you could come by.

אפשר להביא מישהו איתי?
Efshar lehavee mishehoo itee?
Can I bring someone?

כן, בכיף. זה נשמע טוב. באיזו שעה?
Ken, bekef. Zeh nishma tov. Be'eyzo sha'ah?
Yes, sure. Sounds good. At what time?

אני אביא משהו לאכול (לשתות)?
Anee avee mashehoo le'ekhol (lishtot)?
Shall I bring something to eat (drink)?

לצערי אני לא יכול בשבת.
Letsa'aree anee lo yakhol beshabat.
Unfortunately I'm unavailable on Saturday.

לצערי יש לי כבר תוכניות לשבת.
Letsa'aree yesh lee kvar tokhniyot leshabat.
Unfortunately I have plans for Saturday already.

איפה אתה גר?
Eyfo ata gar?
Where do you live?

ברחוב ארלוזורוב 12. זה לא רחוק מהים.
Birkhov Arlozorov shtem-esreh. Zeh lo rakhok mehayam.
At 12 Arlozorov Street. It's not far from the sea.

סבבה, נתראה בשבת.
Sababa, nitra'eh beshabat.
OK, see you on Saturday!

נלך לשתות קפה ביום שני?
Nelekh lishtot kafeh beyom shenee?
Let's go for coffee on Monday.

כן, בטח. מתי ואיפה ניפגש?
Ken, betakh. Matay ve'eyfo nipagesh?
Yes, sure. When and where do we meet?

בארבע בכניסה הראשית של הקניון.
Be'arba baknisah harashit shel hakenyon.
At 4pm at the main entrance of the shopping mall.

משם נלך למדרחוב.
Misham nelekh lamidrekhov.
From there we'll walk to the pedestrian zone.

סגור, להתראות!
Sagoor, lehitra'ot!
Sounds good, see you then!

אתה יודע איפה אפשר לאכול פה פיצה טובה?
Ata yode'a eyfo efshar le'ekhol po pizza tovah?
Do you know where we can find some good pizza?

יש פה באיזור בר נחמד?
Yesh po ba'eyzor bar nekhmad?
Is there a nice bar around here?

כן, אני מכיר אחד. אבוא לאסוף אותך ב-9.
Ken, ani mekeer ekhad. Avo le'esof otkha be-9.
Yes, I know one. I'll pick you up at 9.

סבבה, נתראה יותר מאוחר!
Sababa, nitra'eh yoter me'ookhar!
OK, see you later!

שלום, הגעתם לתא הקולי של אבי כהן.
Shalom, heegatem lata hakolee shel Avi Cohen.
Hello, you have reached the personal voicemail of Avi Cohen.

אני לא יכול לענות כרגע.
Anee lo yakhol la'anot karega.
Unfortunately I'm unable to answer your call at the moment.

אנא השאירו את שמכם ומספר הטלפון אחרי הביפ.
Ana hash'eeroo et shimkhem vemispar hatelefon akhrey habeep.
Please leave your name and phone number after the tone.

אנא השאירו הודעה אחרי הביפ.
Ana hash'eeroo hoda'ah akhrey habeep.
Please leave your message after the tone.

אחזוא אליכם בהקדם האפשרי.
Akhzor eleykhem bahekdem ha'efsharee.
I'll call you back as soon as possible.

תודה שהתקשרתם.
Todah shehitkashartem.
Thank you for calling.

שלום, מדברת יונית. אני מתקשרת בקשר למסיבה בשבת הקרובה.
Shalom, medaberet yoneet. Anee mitkasheret bekesher
lameseebah bashabat hakrovah.
Hi, this is Yonit. I'm calling regarding the party next Saturday.

שלום, מדבר יוסי. אני מתקשר בקשר לפגישה שלנו.
Shalom, medaber Yossi. Anee mitkasher bekesher lapgeeshah
shelanoo.
Hello, this is Yossi. I'm calling regarding our meeting.

אפשר להשיג אותי ב-089123456.

Efshar lehaseeg otee be-089123456.

You can reach me at 089-123456.

אנסה שוב יותר מאוחר.

Anaseh shoov yoter me'ookhar.

I'll try again later.

להתראות. תשמור על עצמך. נתראה אחר כך.

Lehitra'ot. Tishmor al atzmekhah. Nitra'eh akhar kakh.

Good bye! Take care! See you later!

FINAL WORDS

I would like to thank you for purchasing this book and taking huge steps towards becoming a fluent Hebrew speaker!

I really hope that I was able to help you boost your conversation skills and provide you with high quality content that will help you achieve your language learning goals.

The next step for you is to keep speaking Hebrew. A great way to do so is finding a language partner and practice conversation. There are many websites that help you connect with native speakers for free, but I especially like italki.com. I have used it many times for myself and find it very user friendly and professional.

If you enjoyed this book, please could you take 20 seconds to share your positive thoughts and post a review on the Amazon book page? I really appreciate seeing these reviews as it helps spread the word for my work.

Thank you and I wish you all the best for your ongoing language learning journey!

MP3 AUDIO FILES

ACCESS TO THE AUDIO FILES

In order to offer you the best possible learning experience, I created audio files for all the sentences in this book. You can listen to the tracks online, download them or study on the go by using the Soundcloud App. Please type the following link in your browser to access the recordings:

https://soundcloud.com/user-909175221/sets/

Made in United States
North Haven, CT
15 September 2023

41604141R00032